HELLO? IS THIS MR. GRAHAM BELL?

BIOGRAPHY BOOKS FOR KIDS 9-12

CHILDREN'S BIOGRAPHY BOOKS

BABY PROFESSOR

EDUCATION KIDS

Speedy Publishing LLC

40 E. Main St. #1156

Newark, DE 19711

www.speedypublishing.com

Copyright 2017

In this book, we're going to talk about the inventor of the telephone, Alexander Graham Bell. So, let's get right to it!

WHO WAS ALEXANDER GRAHAM BELL?

Alexander Graham Bell was the most important inventor associated with the creation of the telephone. He also did very critical work on communication for people who were deaf. During his lifetime, he obtained over 18 patents for his inventions under his own name and 12 other patents in collaboration with other inventors.

ALEXANDER GRAHAM BELL

EDINBURGH IN SCOTLAND

EARLY LIFE

Alexander was born in March of 1847 in the city of Edinburgh in Scotland. During his early life, both the city where he lived and his family had a profound effect on him. Edinburgh had a culture that was rich with the arts and sciences. Alexander's grandfather and father were doing important work regarding voice mechanics and speech.

They conducted experiments with sound that were designed to provide a form of speech that would be visible for people who couldn't hear. His mother was a master pianist even though she was almost deaf. Her attitude toward challenges inspired the young Alexander. Alexander had two brothers as well, but sadly they both died of tuberculosis at a young age.

ELIZA GRACE SYMONDS BELL

EDUCATION

Alexander's mother, Eliza Grace Symonds Bell, took on the task of teaching Alexander at home and she encouraged his curiosity as well as his problem-solving abilities. He also attended private school for a year and then went on to the Royal High School in Edinburgh where he did two years of study.

He wasn't the best student, but he had an inventive mind and was constantly trying to solve problems that he observed.

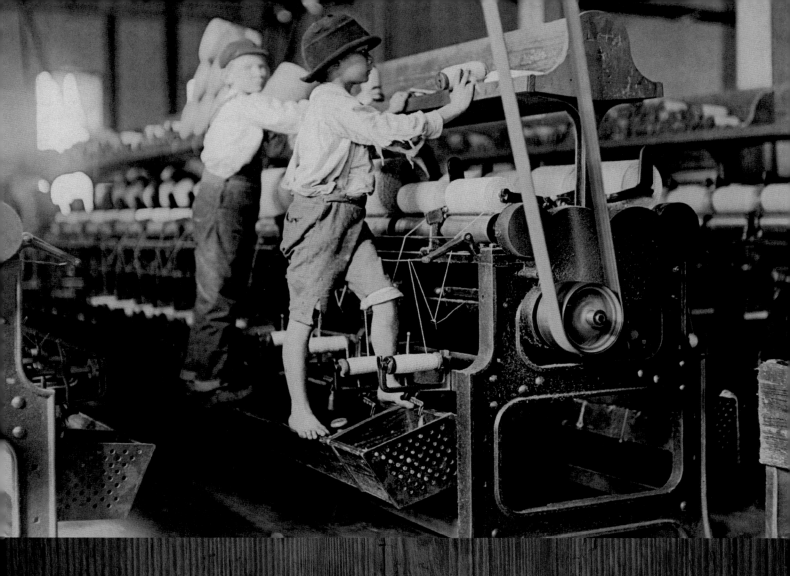

He was playing with one of his friends in a grain mill when he noticed that husking the grains of wheat was a very slow process.

He wondered if there would be a better, quicker way to husk the wheat. He started to experiment at home and constructed a device using paddles that rotated along with brushes to quickly and easily remove the grain husks.

HIS TEENAGE YEARS

Alexander was ambitious and headstrong. His father, Alexander Melville Bell, had a controlling nature, so sometimes the two of them did not get along. His father wanted Alexander to follow in his footsteps, but Alexander was too independent and wanted to be free from the reins of his father. So, in 1862, when Alexander's grandfather became ill, 15-year-old Alexander offered to take care of him.

ALEXANDER GRAHAM BELL

LONDON

Alexander's grandfather had a very positive influence on him. He encouraged Alexander to learn and to continue his intellectual interests. This influence transformed the way Alexander approached his family's work, and he eventually joined his father in his important work. He was still a teenager when he took over the responsibility for the work being done in their London office.

Alexander's father made trips abroad and he discovered that the climate in North America was more to his liking.

He felt that the North American environment was healthier than what his family was experiencing in Europe.

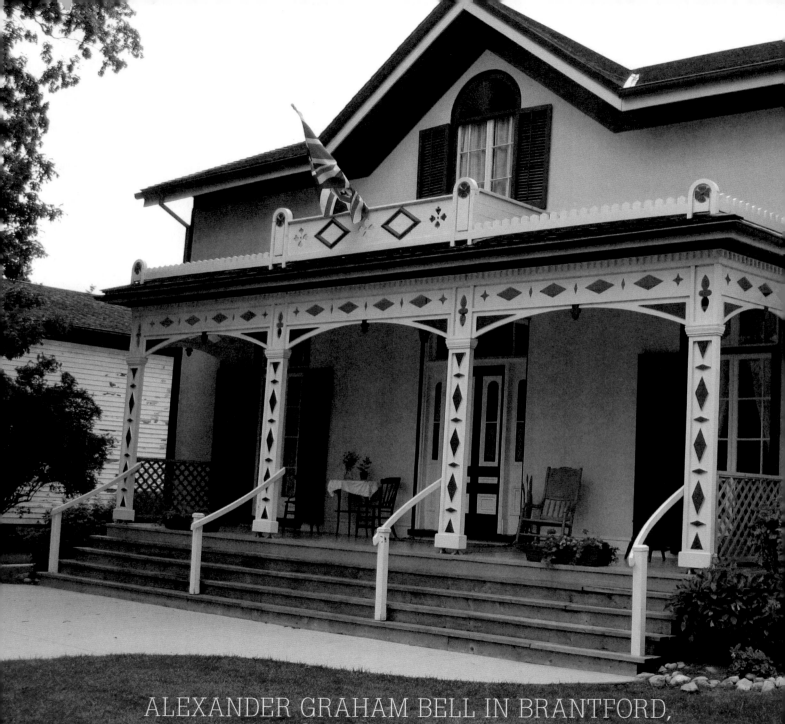

ALEXANDER GRAHAM BELL IN BRANTFORD, ONTARIO, CANADA

Alexander didn't want to make the move because he was establishing his reputation in London, but when his brothers died of tuberculosis, he agreed with his father. In 1870, the Bell family settled in Ontario, Canada. Soon after they arrived, Alexander established a laboratory to continue his studies on voice.

THE INVENTION OF THE TELEPHONE

At the age of twenty-four, Alexander moved to Boston. He started to research the idea of creating an invention that would allow several messages to be sent via telegraph at the same time using different frequencies. He needed an investment to continue his work, so he approached two local investors.

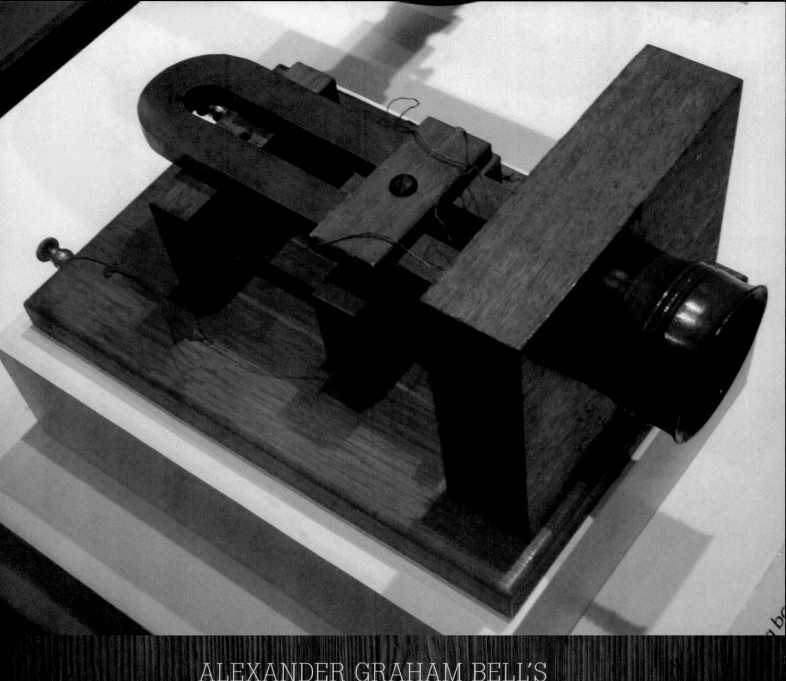

ALEXANDER GRAHAM BELL'S
BIG BOX TELEPHONE, 1876

BELL REED RESONATOR

Gardiner Hubbard agreed to back him and so did Thomas Sanders. From 1873 to 1874, Alexander worked long hours trying to create and perfect this telegraph device, which he had named the "harmonic telegraph." However, while he was working on this invention, he became fascinated by another idea. He started to think about the possibility of sending a human voice from one place to another via wires.

Alexander's financial backers were getting concerned that he wasn't focusing on the original invention that they had agreed to back. To keep him on track, they hired a master electrician by the name of Thomas Watson. Things didn't go as planned.

THOMAS WATSON

THOMAS WATSON

The more Thomas worked with Alexander, the more he realized that Alexander's idea for transmitting voice over wires had vast potential. The two men created an amazing partnership. Alexander was the visionary and idea person and Thomas had the practical experience to help him make his ideas a reality.

For the next year, from 1874 through 1875, the two men worked on both devices. Alexander's investors soon saw the merit of the second invention and a patent was filed to protect it. Then, after much work, on the tenth of March in 1876, they had a breakthrough.

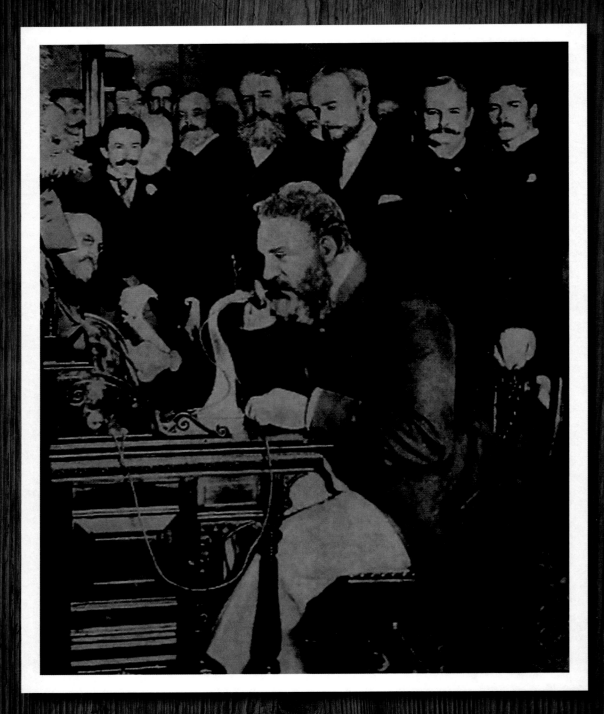

Legend has it that Alexander dropped a container that held fluid used for transmitting and then called out for help from Thomas. However, it's more than likely that Alexander heard some noise coming through the wires and then called out with the now-famous line, "Mr. Watson...come here...I want you!" Thomas Watson was the first person to receive a phone call. The work the two men had done would soon change history.

THE TELEPHONE BECOMES FAMOUS

Now that they had the first working telephone, Alexander began to demonstrate it at public events. In 1876, there was an exhibition in Philadelphia to celebrate the first one hundred years of the United States.

TELEPHONE IN 19TH CENTURY

BELL TELEPHONE COMPANY EMPLOYEES

Dom Pedro, the emperor of the country of Brazil, was in attendance. Alexander demonstrated the telephone to him and Dom Pedro was amazed and exclaimed, "It talks!" With each demonstration, Alexander set up the connecting telephones at further and further distances. In 1877, Alexander's company, the Bell Telephone Company, which is called AT&T today, was founded.

Two days later, Alexander and Mabel Hubbard were married. Mabel was Gardiner Hubbard's daughter and one of Alexander's former students. She was deaf and Alexander had worked with her to teach her to speak. Mabel joined her husband as they went to Europe to demonstrate his new invention.

ALEXANDER GRAHAM BELL
AND FAMILY

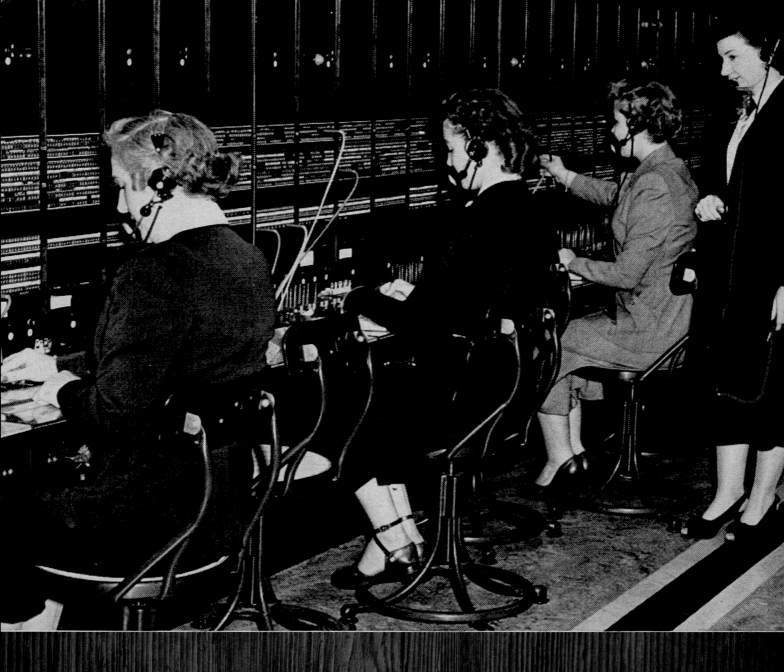

BELL TELEPHONE OPERATORS

COURT CHALLENGES

When Alexander and Mabel returned home from Europe, he had to defend his patent for the telephone in Washington, D.C. Other inventors were claiming that they had come up with the idea before he had. For the next 18 years, there were more than 500 lawsuits brought against the Bell Telephone Company, but in the end Alexander's patent prevailed.

While all these lawsuits were happening, the company continued to get larger. By 1886, more than 150,000 people in the United States had purchased a telephone.

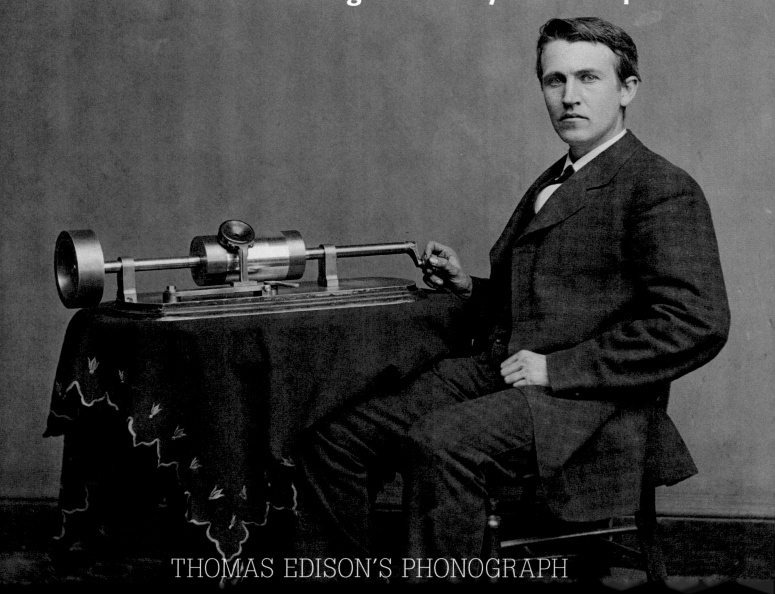

Alexander continued to improve the invention and added a microphone that Thomas Edison had invented so that people could use a regular speaking voice instead of shouting when they used the phone.

THOMAS EDISON'S PHONOGRAPH

1960'S AUDIOMETER

OTHER INVENTIONS BY ALEXANDER GRAHAM BELL

Alexander continued to experiment and conduct research in many scientific areas. He also created other new inventions. Some of the other innovations he was responsible for include:

- A device used for identifying problems with hearing called an **audiometer**.

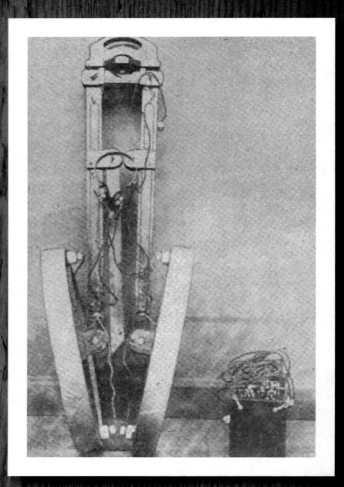

METAL DETECTOR

- A device for detecting metal, which was used on President James Garfield after he was shot in order to identify the location of the bullet

- Experiments with flying devices

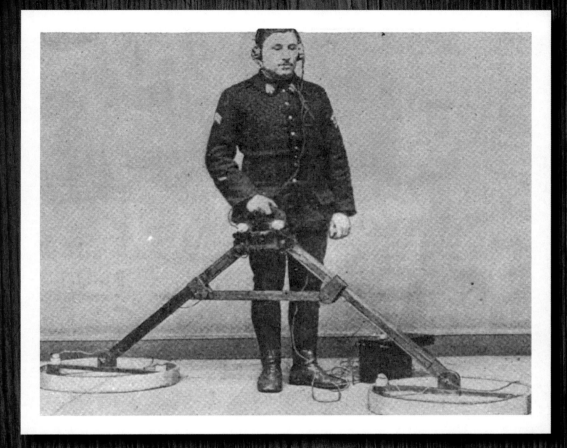

- Experiments on hydrofoils, a type of boat that uses vanes, also called foils, to increase its speed

- Techniques to help train deaf people to speak

- A device used to locate icebergs before they caused damage to ships

BELL AT THE PEMBERTON AVENUE
SCHOOL FOR THE DEAF

HIS FINAL YEARS

Alexander's strength was in creation and in invention, not the day-to-day matters of business. By the year 1880, he had handed over the reins to other managers so he could turn his attention to invention once again. He founded the Volta Laboratory, which was a research institute that was dedicated to science. He also continued to teach deaf pupils and established a special association for this purpose in 1890.

In the last years of his life, Alexander Graham Bell continued to have a hand in numerous projects. He was very interested in building flying machines and he did lots of experiments using the tetrahedral kite beginning in the 1890s.

SIXTEEN CELLED TETRAHEDRAL KITE

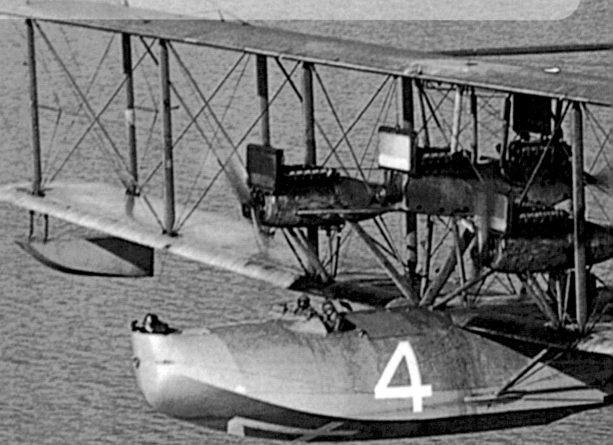

He formed an association called the Aerial Experiment Association with Glenn Curtiss who was one of the very first pilots. Alexander and Glenn along with several other colleagues

CURTISS NC-4 FOUR ENGINE CONFIGURATION

created several different flying machines including a biplane called the Silver Dart, which became the first self-powered airplane flown in Canada.

Later in his career, Alexander worked with hydrofoil boats setting a new record for speed. Alexander lived to see the success of many of his inventions and he became a wealthy man. In 1915, he was asked to make the first phone call from New York to San Francisco.

HYDROFOIL BOAT

ALEXANDER GRAHAM BELL, FIRST
TRANSCONTINENTAL PHONE CALL

He called from New York and his former associate
and friend Thomas Watson answered this
historic call in San Francisco.

When Alexander passed away at the age of 75, the telephone wires were silent for a full minute to honor this great man who was instrumental in how we communicate every day.

Now you know more about the amazing life of Alexander Graham Bell. You can find more Biography books from Baby Professor by searching the website of your favorite book retailer.

Made in the USA
Las Vegas, NV
09 February 2023

67217326R00040